NEW YORK

MASTERPIECES OF ARCHITECTURE

NEW YORK

MASTERPIECES OF ARCHITECTURE

ANDRAS KALDOR

Antique Collectors' Club

Fountain, New York Public Library

To my wife Sally, companion on all my travels,
and our children Nicola, Rupert, Sally, Delia and Jonathan

Special thanks to Mary Hilliard and Leonard Harris my friends and hosts in NY,
Paul Gruber who has been such a help with compiling the list of buildings,
Stevenson B. Andrews for his expertise, and to all those who so generously made
personal contributions to the book.

First published 1999
©1999 Andras Kaldor
World copyright reserved
New edition 2003

ISBN 1 85149 398 0

British Library Cataloguing-in-Publication Data
A catalogue record for this book is available from the British Library

Frontispiece: Solomon R. Guggenheim Museum
Title page: Cooper-Hewitt Museum
Page 96: St. Patrick's Cathedral

Published in England by the Antique Collectors' Club Limited, Woodbridge, Suffolk IP12 4SD
Printed and bound in Italy

Grand Central Terminal (pp.44 and 45)

CONTRIBUTORS

Tracy Byer, banker, page 58

Simon Drew, artist, page 36

Paul Gruber, Executive Director, Metropolitan
Opera Guild, pages 49 and 72

Leonard Harris, author, page 66

Mary Hilliard, photographer, page 45

Al Hirschfeld, artist and caricaturist, page 46

Louise Kerz Hirschfeld, theater historian, page 52

John Loring, Design Director, Tiffany & Co., page 50

Paul Palmer, author, page 14

Deborah Remington, artist, page 85

Demetra Ryder Runton, architect, page 87

George C. Spelvin, theater critic, page 70

Diana Steel, publisher, page 56

The circled numbers
correspond to those
shown in the
building headings

CONTENTS

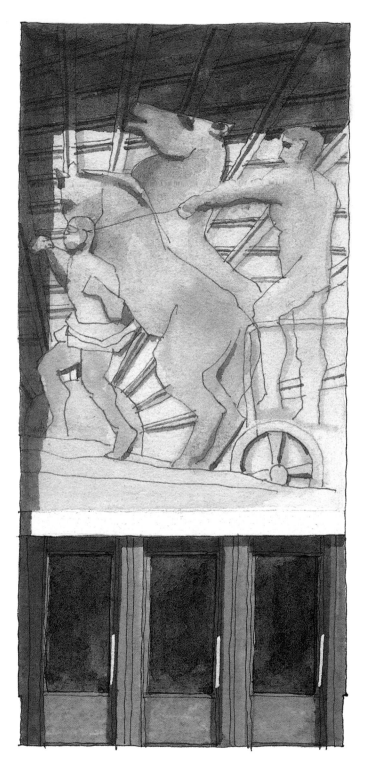

Rockefeller Center

An early New York coat-of-arms

INTRODUCTION

...to a companion for a walk around the famous and
exciting buildings of Manhattan

This little book is designed to take you around Manhattan, and to show you some of the splendid architecture of the city. The great churches, the world famous museums, the old and new headquarters of the big corporations, the public buildings of the city administrators, the places of entertainment and learning, and the great houses built by the industrialists that have now become museums for their and other collections.

The gracious buildings we now find so fascinating were mostly built in the late 19th and early 20th century by proud city fathers and rich entrepreneurs. This great building boom, the result of wealth and new building techniques, forms the core of this great American city.

New York at its best is a splendid example of the marriage of old and new, and this exciting mixture is what makes New York New York the magnet for visitors from all over the world, who come to marvel at the bravery of its skyscrapers, the unforgettable skyline, and the deep valleys of the avenues.

The diversity of architectural styles we see today is guarded by the New York City Landmarks Commission. Since its creation in 1965 it has been responsible for the protection of the city's historic buildings and cultural heritage.

Rockefeller Center

I have been visiting New York for some years now, but still remember the excitement of the approach over the Brooklyn Bridge on the way into Manhattan from JFK airport. One of my recent visits was for an exhibition at the Metropolitan Opera Gallery at the Lincoln Center, where the original paintings from my book the *Opera Houses of Europe* were on show. It was during this trip that the idea of a book about the buildings of Manhattan was first suggested. With my background in architecture, the opportunity to paint the buildings of NY was a commission I accepted enthusiastically.

It has given me the chance to spend more time in the city and to sketch and photograph the buildings, and to research their history and find and persuade New Yorkers to add their personal impressions and anecdotes about the buildings illustrated. I am very lucky to have generous and hospitable friends living in the city, kind enough to show me around their town. Their knowledge and enthusiasm has made the task of putting this book together a thoroughly enjoyable one.

In discovering New York, the next best thing to intelligent and enthusiastic friends is this little book. I wish you happy wandering with it, and hope you will enjoy your walks as much as I have.

Andras Kaldor
New York, May 1999

Entrance to the Ansonia Hotel

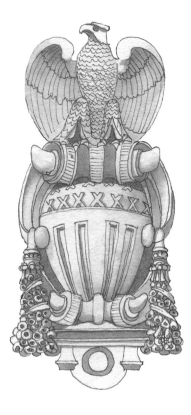

1. ELLIS ISLAND
IMMIGRANT RECEIVING STATION

There are places where the structure of the building is of little significance, so overwhelming is the history behind it. The Immigrant Receiving Station which occupies virtually the whole of Ellis Island is one such place. By the time the station finally closed its doors in 1954 millions of immigrants had passed through its halls on their way into the United States.

The present buildings were erected in one year after a fire destroyed the previous timber structures. The small firm of architects, Boring and Tilton, won the contract to design the new station in 1898, and the main building was opened in December 1900. Contemporary accounts described the building as "an imposing as well as pleasing addition to the picturesque waterfront of the metropolis". The main receiving and registry station has a French Renaissance exterior of brick and limestone with imposing towers at the corners. Of the constant arrivals, most passed quickly through the formalities and were on their way to New York City and beyond.

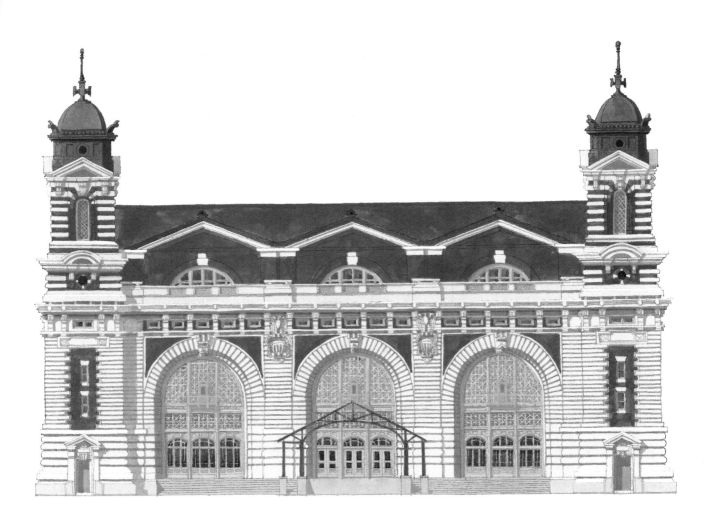

Some, however, were detained in dormitories for thorough health checks, while a small percentage were returned to their port of embarkation. The original buildings were soon enlarged to accommodate a proper hospital, and landfill was required to further enlarge the complex to deal with the rising number of arrivals.

After the closure of the island in 1954, the buildings suffered from neglect, until, in 1965, the island was declared part of the Statue of Liberty National Monument. Restoration began in 1983, and the Ellis Island Immigration Museum opened in September 1990.

Architects Boring and Tilton
Opened 1900

2. STATUE OF LIBERTY
LIBERTY ISLAND

The Statue of Liberty, known the world over as the symbol of the United States of America, was a gift from the people of France. The colossal statue is the creation of the Alsatian sculptor, Bartholdi, who started work on it in 1871.

French intellectuals advocating republican rule, hoped that the construction of such a statue would help spread democracy in France, and unite France and the United States in a common quest for freedom and liberty. Money was raised in France, and construction began in 1875. Gustave Eiffel designed the wrought iron armature to withstand the elements in New York harbor and to support the beaten copper exterior.

The 154 foot high pedestal on which the statue stands was designed by Richard Morris Hunt, a French trained architect, and was built of Stony Creek granite and concrete. Funds for the base were raised by the *New York World* newspaper and its proprietor Joseph Pulitzer.

The 151-foot-tall statue arrived from France in hundreds of cases in 1885 and was dedicated on Bedloe's Island on October 28, 1886. The date of the Declaration of Independence, July 4, 1776, is inscribed on the tablet carried in the left hand of the figure.

A BRILLIANT VISION
It was my first trip to New York. The mid-1980s, the height of the Decade of Greed, and I was there for a banker's wedding on the Upper East Side. On the flight over we had endured five hours of terrifying turbulence; but then, as the TWA plane banked to the right, the clouds suddenly opened up. And there, in the late-afternoon sunshine, granite and gold brilliantly ablaze, her flame seeming to reach up to us 2,000 feet above her, was the Statue. As the child of Irish immigrants, I thought of those who'd arrived at Ellis Island by sea and glanced across at Bedloe's and seen her for the first time. Then, they had gazed up at her magnificence; I peered down, equally in awe. I only saw her once more on that rain-sodden trip: from the Port Authority steps on the day I was leaving, shrouded in a mist as fine as muslin, as if she was saving herself for other first-timers.   *Paul Palmer, author*

Sculptor Frédéric Auguste Bartholdi; Engineer Gustave Eiffel
Unveiled 1886

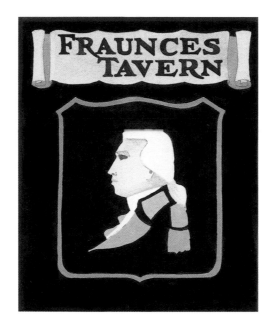

3. FRAUNCES TAVERN
54 PEARL STREET

The present building stands on the site of a private home built in 1719 by Stephen DeLancey. The original building was turned into a tavern by a West Indian Creole named Samuel Fraunces, who later became George Washington's steward. It was in this tavern that Washington gave the farewell speech to his officers, on December 4, 1783, after winning the war against the British. Subsequently the building suffered several fires, and in the course of time was enlarged from three stories to five. In 1904 the building was bought by the Sons of the Revolution, who commissioned William Mersereau to reconstruct it. The Colonial Revival design is largely guesswork by the architect but it is nevertheless a pleasing structure. Fraunces Tavern now homes a restaurant with wood-burning fireplaces on the ground floor, and a museum on the upper floors.

Architect William Mersereau
Built 1719, restored 1907

4. United States Custom House

Bowling Green

The former Custom House was designed by the Minnesota architect Cass Gilbert in a masterful Beaux-Arts style. Built between 1892 and 1907, this large quadrangular building reflects the contemporary importance of the City of New York as the principal port of the nation.

The many sculptures decorating the facade represent trade and commerce. The cartouche above the main entrance, of two winged figures either side the shield of the United States and an eagle with spread wings, is the work of the sculptor Karl Bitter. The four large seated female figures by Daniel Chester French represent America, Asia, Europe and Africa.

The building now houses the George Gustav Heye Center of the National Museum of the American Indian of the Smithsonian Institution. The collection, assembled in the first half of the 20th century by G.G. Heye, forms the cornerstone of this Museum, exhibiting some one million Indian artifacts from North, South and Central America.

Architect Cass Gilbert
Built 1892–1907

5. NEW YORK STOCK EXCHANGE
8 BROAD STREET

Trading in stocks and shares has taken place in and around Wall Street since 1792, when the first traders met under a buttonwood tree in this street. The present building was designed by George B. Post who acquired his Beaux-Arts training in the offices of Richard Morris Hunt in the 1850s. Built in 1901–3, Post was 63 years old when he started work on what was to be the most memorable building of his career. The unusual two-story-high base to the columns has arched doorways opening on to massively supported balconies, all in white marble. The six 52-feet-high Corinthian columns supporting the pediment are but a screen to the glazed wall lighting the great trading hall. The pediment is filled with sculptures, designed by John Quincy Adams Ward and sculpted by Paul W. Bartlett. The sculptures you see now are copies in lead, coated to resemble the original marble figures damaged by the city's atmosphere.

Architect George B. Post
Built 1901–1903

6. FEDERAL HALL

28 WALL STREET

Built between 1832 and 1842 as the United States Custom House, it later became the Federal Reserve Bank before being listed as a National Monument in 1939.

It is one of finest classical designs in the City in Greek Revival style with fluted Doric columns supporting an unadorned pediment and surmounting a flight of steps. The marble for its construction was quarried a few miles outside the city.

An imposing bronze statue of George Washington on the steps marks the spot where the nation's first president took his oath of office in 1789. On each side of the steps bronze plaques also refer to this occasion. However, the famous event predates the building by over forty years; the original building where the historic oath was taken was demolished in 1812.

Today the building is the Museum of American Constitutional Government.

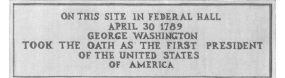

ON THIS SITE IN FEDERAL HALL
APRIL 30 1789
GEORGE WASHINGTON
TOOK THE OATH AS THE FIRST PRESIDENT
OF THE UNITED STATES
OF AMERICA

Architects Town & Davis, S. Thompson, W. Ross and J. Frazee
Built 1832–1842

ON THIS SITE IN FEDERAL HALL
APRIL 30 1789
GEORGE WASHINGTON
TOOK THE OATH AS THE FIRST PRESIDENT
OF THE UNITED STATES
OF AMERICA

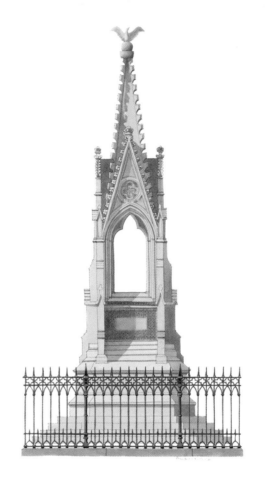

7. TRINITY CHURCH
BROADWAY AT WALL STREET

This was one of the first Gothic Revival buildings in New York and one of the earliest works of the architect Richard Upjohn, the founder of the American Institute of Architects. Built between 1839 and 1846, the structure was the tallest in the city for nearly 50 years, with the spire towering 281 feet over the surrounding business district. The present building is the third one on this site for New York's oldest Episcopal congregation, the original church having been founded in 1696.

Built of New Jersey brownstone, the exterior was cleaned in 1990, removing the black grime of years to reveal the original varied coloring of the stone.

The surrounding graveyard contains the gravestones of many famous Americans including Alexander Hamilton, Albert Gallatin and William Bradford, and features many fine 18th century gravestones.

Architect Richard Upjohn
Built 1839–1846

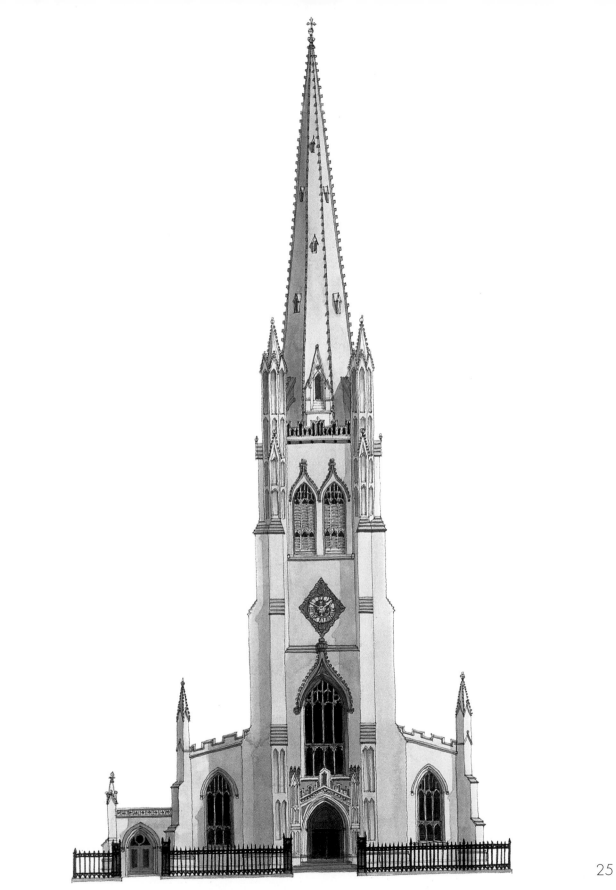

8. CITY HALL
CITY HALL PARK

Joseph Mangin, a French émigré, and John McComb, a Scotsman, submitted the winning competition design for City Hall in 1802. Completed in 1812, it has been the seat of New York City government ever since.

City Hall is regarded as one of the finest examples of early 19th century American architecture. Its elegant symmetrical facade is redolent of French Renaissance influence with a central portico topped by a cupola clock tower and flanked by two projecting wings, whilst the interior is Neo-classical Georgian with a fine domed rotunda encircled by ten columns crowning an elegant double curving marble stairway.

Curiously, although the front of the building was originally clad in white marble, the rear was left unclad as it faced north and, at the time of its erection, it was thought unlikely that anyone would ever either need or wish to reside on that side. It was only as the result of public outcry that the northern side was faced with white marble in 1954.

Henry James eulogized its "perfect taste and finish, the reduced, yet ample scale, the harmony of the parts, the just proportions, the modest classic grace".

Architects Joseph Mangin and John McComb Jr.
Opened 1812

9. WOOLWORTH BUILDING
233 BROADWAY

When Frank W. Woolworth decided to build the headquarters for his company he seemed to know exactly what he wanted and where in the city the building should be. His choice was to be the Gothic Revival Style with Cass Gilbert, who had recently designed the U.S. Customs House (pp.18 and 19), as architect. The building was to be the tallest in the world, a distinction it retained until 1930 when the Chrysler Building was opened.

To realize this immense project a company was set up with the Irving National Bank arranging the finance. The land was acquired, Cass Gilbert was appointed, plans were drawn up and modified until the final design of 30 stories and a 25-story tower was approved. The most experienced firm of builders was hired for the construction work and the finest materials were used for the fitting and finishes. An indication of the perfectionism of Woolworth is found in his insistence that the decorative elements on the exterior of the building should extend not just to the front, but also to the sides and rear.

The building was opened in 1913 with President Woodrow Wilson switching on the lights from his office in the White House. The skyscraper proved a winner even in financial terms: just one year after the opening, Woolworth was able to buy back all the shares in the company set up to build it.

The critics and newspapers of the time declared the building to be "imperturbably august, a conquest of architecture".

Architect Cass Gilbert
Completed 1913

10. MANHATTAN BRIDGE ARCH
MANHATTAN BRIDGE AT CANAL STREET

Plans for this triumphal archway were not put in hand until after the bridge itself had opened in 1909. The imposing archway and its twin curving colonnades were designed by Carrère and Hastings. They now offer a monumental gateway to the Manhattan end of the bridge, one of the main links to Brooklyn. The frieze above the arch is by Charles Rumsey; depicting a buffalo hunt, it seems rather a strange subject in its urban setting. The reliefs above the doorways on either side of the arch depict the Spirit of Commerce on the left hand side and the Spirit of Industry on the right.

The Brooklyn end of the bridge approach was lost to highway improvement, while the Manhattan end is being restored.

Architects Carrère and Hastings
Built 1910–1915

11. St. Mark's-in-the-Bowery Church
Second Avenue at East 10th Street

The second oldest church building in Manhattan is built on the site of a private chapel on the farm of the Dutch governor, Peter Stuyvesant, who is buried in the churchyard. The site was sold for $1 by the governor's great grandson to the Episcopal Church.

The church, with a simple pediment, was built around 1799. The Greek revival steeple, designed by Town and Thompson, was added in 1828, making the church the most prominent building in the East Village at the time. The cast iron portico is from 1854.

As the surrounding area and the community changed over time the church became neglected, until in 1975 a restoration project involving local residents was put in hand. In spite of a bad fire in 1978, the task was completed in 1983.

Architects Town and Thompson
Built circa 1799

12. JEFFERSON MARKET LIBRARY
425 SIXTH AVENUE

This Victorian Gothic edifice was threatened with demolition in the 1950s and it was only thanks to the unremitting efforts of a conservation group, who campaigned to have the building turned into a public library, that it was saved from the wrecker's ball. The New York Public Library agreed to take it over in 1961 and the building re-opened in its new role in 1967.

It was originally built in the 1870s as a courthouse with the encircling balcony half way up the bell tower serving as a fire watch tower. The bell itself was used to summon volunteer firemen.

The red brick building has an elaborately ornamented facade with fanciful decorations including a pediment depicting the trial scene from *The Merchant of Venice*.

Architects Vaux & Withers
Built 1874–1877

13. FLATIRON BUILDING

175 FIFTH AVENUE AT BROADWAY

The Flatiron Building was one of the first steel-framed structures, and every aspect of the revolutionary features of this new medium was taken into consideration. No traditional masonry building could have been as slender and reached such a height in 1902, the year it was completed. Standing 286 feet high, it was the tallest building in the world.

In form, however, it retained very much the style of its time with a limestone facing hiding its steel frame and giving it the overtones of an Italianate palazzo.

Its location at the junction of Fifth Avenue and Broadway dictated its distinctive wedge shape which in turn was to give it its name. Originally named the Fuller Building, it was not long before it was renamed the Flatiron Building.

Its remarkably slim shape, with a width of only 6 feet at the apex, raised initial fears that the building would prove unstable and would soon be demolished by the wind. Such fears proved unfounded and, nearly a century on, like the prow of some enormous oncoming vessel, it continues to tower over the busy intersection of two great avenues.

MY BIGGEST SURPRISE

Illustrations of the Flatiron Building cannot prepare you for the shock you receive as your taxi zips past it. The extraordinary shape is exaggerated by viewing it from a low angle. This makes it even more like the bow of a ship and makes you realize that a madman must have designed a shape to fit a ground plan caused by the vagaries of an Indian trail. Of all the famous buildings in New York, this is the most unexpected and is lodged in my heart sideways.

Simon Drew, artist

Architect D.H. Burnham & Co.
Built 1901–1903

14. Pierpont Morgan Library

33 East 36th Street

The library was constructed in 1902, in the quiet district of Murray Hill, for the financier J. Pierpont Morgan to house his collection of rare books and manuscripts. The design was by the architectural firm of McKim, Mead & White. The main feature of the building is the facade with a Palladian arch between Ionic columns and Tuscan pilasters. The walls are in solid Knoxville marble, laid without mortar.

Two sculptured panels by Andrew O'Connor represent Tragic Poetry and Lyric Poetry. The lions on either side of the steps are by Edward Clark Potter, who also sculpted the lions at the New York Public Library (pp.42 and 43). In 1928, after the death of Pierpont Morgan, an addition to the west of the library was built in Classical Revival style by Benjamin Wistar Morris. The glass pavilion at the rear was added in 1991 by Voorsanger Mills. Of the three rooms in the original building, the West Library, formerly Morgan's study, is considered "one of the great achievements of American interior decoration".

Architects McKim, Mead & White
Built 1902

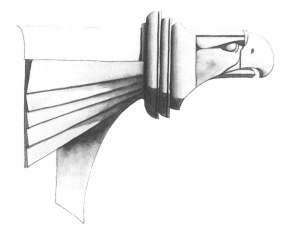

15. CHRYSLER BUILDING
LEXINGTON AVENUE AT 42ND STREET

Walter P. Chrysler founded the motor car company which bears his name in 1925 and it was not long before he decided to create a New York headquarters for his burgeoning company. The classic Art Deco building which transpired drew much of its decorative inspiration from the motor car, particularly from stylised radiator grilles, hub caps, and hood ornaments.

Its distinctive stainless steel pinnacle was based on the radiator cap of the 1930 Chrysler car, while the gargoyles were inspired by hood ornaments from the 1929 Chrysler Plymouth.

The crowning spire was assembled in great secrecy within the upper stories of the building, and was finally raised to its present position in 1930, making the Chrysler building the tallest building in the world and the first building to exceed the height of the Eiffel Tower. However, this 77-story building was not to enjoy this distinction for long: within 18 months the Empire State Building was completed.

Inside there is a sumptuous lobby which was restored in 1978. It features Cubist patterned marbles and granites with chrome trims and a painted ceiling by Edward Trumball showing transportation and industrial scenes.

Today the Chrysler Building is one of the best known and most easily recognizable of Manhattan landmarks.

Architect William Van Alen
Built 1928–1930

16. NEW YORK PUBLIC LIBRARY

476 FIFTH AVENUE

This library, arguably the greatest Beaux-Arts masterpiece of architecture in the United States, was opened by President William Howard Taft in 1911.

The John Jacob Astor, James Lenox and Samuel Tilden foundations combined in 1895 to donate their own libraries to, and finance the establishment of, the Public Library. Construction work began in 1902. The founding benefactors are commemorated in carved tablets above the main entrance, separated by six sculpted figures by Paul Wayland Bartlett.

The library was built on land owned by the city and constructed of Dorset white marble from Vermont to the design of architects Carrère and Hastings. Although the scale of the building is very large it is not overpowering. The triple arch of the central entrance pavilion is flanked by fountains by Frederick MacMonnies, and the entry from the sidewalk is guarded by a pair of reclining lions (sometimes known as Patience and Fortitude) by Edward C. Potter.

The library, one of the largest in the world, is for reference only. Entrance is free.

Architects Carrère and Hastings
Built 1902–1911

17. Grand Central Terminal

Park Avenue at 42nd Street

Grand Central is one of the world's great railway terminals, and an outstanding example of Beaux-Arts design by the architects Warren and Wetmore. The partnership of Reed and Stem was responsible for the innovative layout of the complex, aided by the engineer William J. Wilgus.

The terminal was financed by Cornelius Vanderbilt's New York Railroad Company; his statue stands below the main facade. It was opened in 1913.

The steel frame of the building is clad in granite and limestone. The three imposing arched windows on the south elevation are separated by pairs of Doric columns. Above the central arch is the 13-foot clock adorned with a sculpture of Mercury, Hercules and Minerva. The vast vaulted space of the beautifully proportioned interior handles some 200,000 commuters a day. The high domed ceiling is decorated by a painting of the celestial constellations by Paul Helleu.

The recently restored and cleaned Terminal deserves to be on any itinerary: its size and complexity indicate its importance in an age when the railway was the principal means of transport.

SCHOOL OUTING

Each time I walk through Grand Central I'm 17 again. The grime is gone now, whisked away by a wonderful renovation, but the lofty, star-sprinkled ceiling is the same. So are the hurrying people, and the domed passage outside the Oyster Bar where you can whisper in one corner and be heard in another. We'd arrive from boarding school, and Grand Central was our gateway to the heady adventures of New York City . . . not to the museum visits our school had in mind, but to Saks and Bonwit's and the underground passageway between the station and the Roosevelt Hotel's Rough Rider Room where, with some U. Va. boys, we giddily caroused chanting "I Think We Need Another Drink", and the platform we raced along, frantically puffing on forbidden cigarettes, to catch the last train back to school. Seventeen and the Rough Rider Room are gone. But the memories and the thrill – never.

Mary Hilliard, photographer

Architects Warren and Wetmore
Opened 1913

18. NEW VICTORY THEATER

209 WEST 42ND STREET

Originally named the Republic, this playhouse opened in September 1900. It was the seventh theater project of Oscar Hammerstein who described it as "the perfect parlor theater, compact in size, artistic in decoration, and complete in every detail . . . a drawing room of the drama, dedicated to all that is best in dramatic and lyric art".

In 1931, at a time when many theaters were changing over to movies, the Republic converted to modern burlesque from Billy Minsky, the most famous purveyor of striptease. This remained the main fare at the Republic until 1942 when, in a burst of wartime patriotism, the name of the theater was changed to the New Victory Theater and it began showing movies; it continued to do so until its closure for restoration in the early 1990s, when it benefited from over $11 million dollars from a fund provided by the City and State.

The New Victory opened in December 1995 as a full-time theater for children and families, retaining its position as Times Square's oldest existing theater.

IF BUILDINGS COULD TALK...

The New Victory Theater, having survived two World Wars, the Depression and the beginning of a new age of computers, would certainly remember, early last century, the horse-drawn carriage line at the corner of 42nd Street and Broadway just around the corner from the Rialto Theater. The wonderful opening night audiences dressed in corseted evening gowns and top-hatted escorts. The Flea Circus and the New Amsterdam Theater across the street. The Times Square and Apollo Theaters down the block where George Gershwin played pit piano for *George White's Scandals* at the Apollo. The smell of perfume and horse manure permeating the atmosphere. The critics bolting out of their aisle seats and rushing back to their newspapers to make the early editions which were on the street by 1 a.m. Their reviews read aloud at Sardi's Restaurant just around the corner from the *New York Times*.

All and more would be accurately recorded if only the New Victory Theater could talk. *Al Hirschfeld, artist and caricaturist*

Architects J.B.McElsatrick 1900; Hardy, Holzman & Pfeiffer 1995
Opened 1900; restored, reopened 1995

19. FORD CENTER FOR THE PERFORMING ARTS

Formerly the Lyric Theatre
213 WEST 42ND STREET

The composer and impresario Reginald DeKoven, after 13 years of touring the country with his very popular and profitable musical, *Robin Hood*, decided to settle down and invest the considerable earnings he had made on the road in a new theater. A site on 42nd Street, owned by the Shubert brothers, was purchased and the beautiful Lyric was built in 1903 to the design of V. Hugo Koehler. The theater's two grand entrances provide easy access to the auditorium; an iron and glass canopy protects the one on 42nd Street, and the other, illustrated, on 43rd Street, is decorated in the classical mode with theatrical masks, lyres and muses.

From October 1903, when Richard Mansfield opened the theater with *Old Heidelberg*, until 1905 when Douglas Fairbanks starred in *Fontana*, the Shubert brothers worked together until the death of Sam Shubert in 1905. After that Lee and J.J. continued and built an empire that greatly influenced the Broadway theater. Successful runs of shows continued until 1934 when the theater became a movie house. It was closed in 1992.

The Ford Center for the Performing Arts bought the Lyric and the adjacent Apollo and, combining these into one, created a splendid theatrical environment, the second largest seating over 1800 people in comfort. The new theater was inaugurated in December 1997 with the Tony Award winning Broadway premier of *Ragtime*.

Architect V. Hugo Koehler
Built 1903

THE CHANGING LYRIC

The Lyric holds a peculiar position among New York's playhouses: it exists, but it doesn't. Walk along 43rd Street and you'll find a handsomely restored facade, compared by many to an Italian Renaissance mansion, with "Lyric Theatre" carved in white marble. Behind that facade is a fully functioning theater, but its auditorium has little to do with the old Lyric that opened in 1903, and played host to the likes of Fred and Adele Astaire and the Marx Brothers.

   As part of the ballyhooed '42nd Street Revitalization', the Lyric and its neighbor the Apollo were gutted in the mid-1990s, and a new theater, the Ford Center for the Performing Arts, created within the outer walls of the old buildings. The new Times Square is cleaner and infinitely more tourist-friendly. But the Ford Center, or at least its interior, is the perfect symbol for what Times Square has become: sterile, artificial, a counterfeit restoration – theater as a merchandising opportunity. Redevelopment has become over-development, and the theater district now looks like a cross between Las Vegas and a mega-mall. *Paul Gruber, Executive Director, Metropolitan Opera Guild*

20. NEW YORK YACHT CLUB
37 WEST 44TH STREET

At the end of the 19th century the New York Yacht Club was the haunt of fabulously wealthy owners of steam and racing yachts which competed with each other in size and magnificence. The original club house was on Madison Avenue. When it became necessary to find new premises J. Pierpont Morgan purchased and donated the land on which the Club was to be built.

A number of architectural firms were asked to submit designs. Warren and Wetmore, who happened also to be members, incorporated significant elements of naval architecture into their winning proposal. The facade of the building features Poseidon, the Sea God, as well as maritime devices such as anchors and ropes. Even the shape of the bay windows echoes the stern shapes of Dutch sailing vessels or *jachts*.

The Club opened in 1900 with a glittering reception to which ladies were invited – thus breaking a strictly enforced Club rule that insisted on it being a male preserve.

IN THE ADMIRAL'S QUARTERS

In 1954 my mother married four-star, 'fighting' Admiral J.J. Clark. By then he had left his flagship *The Yorktown* behind for a quieter life in New York City, where his flagship was one of the three carved limestone galleons whose sterns ornament the extravagantly elaborate Beaux-Arts facade of the New York Yacht Club on West 44th Street. The family would sit in these grandiose, if makeshift, Admiral's quarters on a regular basis, and at cocktail time listen to the Admiral sail through the long-since-charted waters of his naval triumphs in World War II and Korea. Mother's and the Admiral's assorted children, more than familiar with those stories of better forgotten wars, would let their eyes and daydreams wander into the baronial Renaissance Revival splendor of the club's cavernous model room, which mother would remind us was not at all as ancient as it appeared, having been built in the year of her birth, 1900.

I can never walk by the New York Yacht Club but my eyes wander up to the stone galleon nearest the entrance and I imagine mother and the Admiral forever enthroned in that glorious caprice of architecture that suited them both so well.   *John Loring, Design Director, Tiffany & Co.*

Architects Warren and Wetmore
Opened 1900

51

21. LYCEUM THEATER
149 WEST 45TH STREET

Judged to be the most imposing Beaux-Arts facade in the Broadway theater district, the Lyceum was built for the impresario Daniel Frohman. The architectural firm of Herts and Tallant designed the theater, which opened in 1903 with the production of *The Proud Prince*.

The new Lyceum Theater was deliberately sited on a side street, far enough from Broadway for tranquillity, yet close to Times Square and the new subway. Laying the cornerstone of the new building, Frohman included 13 bricks from the old building for luck.

The design included an apartment, offices, a banquet hall and a directors' room with a view of the stage. The auditorium occupies only about one third of the total space. The rehearsal room has identical curtains and lighting to the main stage, allowing two rehearsals to take place at the same time. The rest of the building houses the set builders, wardrobe store and dressing rooms.

The unparalleled list of stars who have performed there includes, among others, Ethel Barrymore, Bette Davis, Joseph Cotton, Montgomery Clift, Lauren Bacall and Alan Bates.

THE THEATER CHANGED MY LIFE

Here in New York City, a political science major at Queen's College, my goal was to become a history teacher. But fate intervened around my twentieth birthday in the form of an invitation to the theater for the first time. The marvelous building exterior held my attention as did the grand staircase to the second floor, which afforded a closer view of the interior, ceiling and various decorations.

The Lyceum interior became a spiritual place for me. It opened new vistas, I felt the joy and pain of the characters along with the rest of the audience. It was an illuminating experience and in some mystical way I felt comfortable. Which accounts for the fact that I eventually became a theater historian.

Louise Kerz Hirschfeld, theater historian

Architects Herts and Tallant
Opened 1903

53

22. Helmsley Building

230 Park Avenue

Sponsored by the New York Central Railroad company, the building was designed by the architects Warren and Wetmore as offices for the railroads using the Grand Central Terminal. The same architects were also responsible for the design of the railroad terminal. Construction took place between 1927 and 1929.

For a time the tower dominated Park Avenue with its highly decorated roof, but then the taller Pan Am Building, now the Met Life Building, was erected in 1963 behind it.

At ground level, arched openings give access to Grand Central Terminal (pp.44 and 45). The clock above the entrance doors echoes the one over the large windows on the south elevation of the railway terminal itself.

Originally the New York Central Building, it became the Helmsley Building in 1977.

Architects Warren and Wetmore
Built 1927–1929

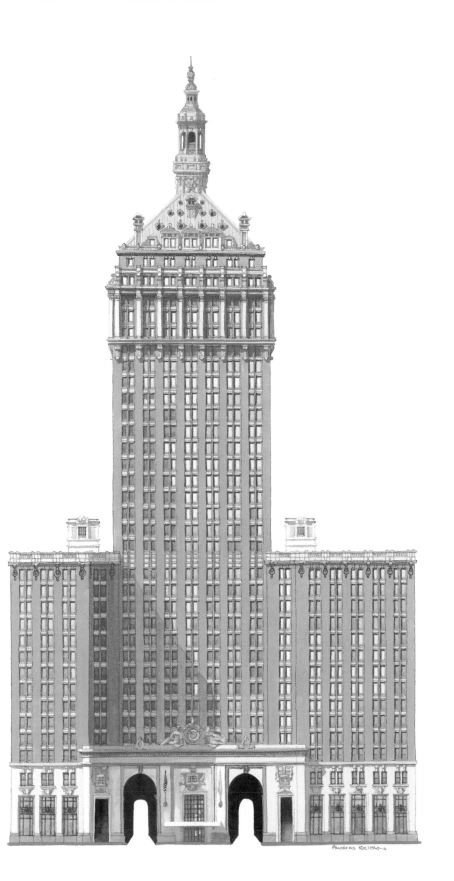

Andras Kaldor

23. CHARLES SCRIBNERS SONS BUILDING
597 FIFTH AVENUE

The building was designed by Ernest Flagg, the Scribners' favorite architect, who, by following the style of earlier work done for the company, established an identifiable image for the firm. Constructed in 1912–13, the building was considered one of the few aesthetically pleasing business structures in the then fashionable Midtown district.

The 10-story limestone-faced building reflects the influence of Paris where Flagg had studied. The metal framed two-story shop window is the most distinguished feature of the facade as befits such a prestigious bookstore. Inside, under a high ceiling, a bookshelf lined balcony was to be found. Sadly the bookstore is no longer and the premises are now occupied by Benetton.

ART NOUVEAU BOOKSTORE
When I first saw this wonderful Art Nouveau building in the late 1970s, it was as a young publisher selling books to Mr Kropotkin, the doyen of New York bookselling and chief buyer for Doubleday Bookstores, who sat just behind the small round window on the right above the main door. The interior of the bookstore had a gallery with small offices for the buyers, positioned so that they could all look down on the sales floors, a wonderfully decorated Art Nouveau extravagance.   *Diana Steel, publisher*

Architect Ernest Flagg
Built 1912–1913

24. ROCKEFELLER CENTER

FIFTH AND SIXTH AVENUES
BETWEEN 47TH AND 50TH STREETS

The Rockefeller Center is spread over two avenues and several streets and the huge 21-acre complex, opposite Saint Patrick's Cathedral, is hard to miss

The original intention for the site was for a new home for the Metropolitan Opera. In 1928 John D. Rockefeller Jr. agreed to lease the land for the project but the Stock Market crashed spectacularly shortly afterwards and the Metropolitan Opera Company withdrew from the scheme. Rockefeller decided to develop the site on his own and, in the years of the Depression, 14 buildings were erected to Art Deco designs. The first tenants came from the young radio and television industry and included RCA, RKO and NBC. The project was conceived as a mixed business center and now, in a total of 19 buildings, it provides office space, stores, restaurants, theaters and garages.

The centerpiece of the complex, the GE Building, was originally called the RCA Building after its main tenant. The slim building soars to a height of 850 feet with its vertical columns of limestone framing the seemingly endless lines of windows.

The architecture of the complex is notable for the abundance of fine art both inside and outside the buildings. Sculpture, mosaics, murals, metalwork and enamels all abound. Amongst them is the Art Deco statue of Atlas carrying the heavens on his shoulders as his punishment for defying Zeus (see page 10).

CHRISTMAS TIME
For the last 30 years or so, every Christmas my family has met at the Rockefeller Center. I can't remember now how the tradition started, but it must have been as a treat for us children, to see the tall Christmas tree, the lights and the angels over the skating rink.

It has been so ever since, and we gather every year from all corners of the world to meet and to spend a special evening together, to catch up on family news and to recapture the magic of those childhood days. Occasionally we still put on skates and always take family photographs recording the growing and changing group that is my family.   *Tracy Byer, banker*

Architects: Associated Architects led by Raymond Hood
Built 1931–1940

25. ST. BARTHOLOMEW'S CHURCH

PARK AVENUE AT 50TH STREET

Set in a terraced garden amid the corporate towers on Fifth Avenue, designed by Bertram Goodhue and built between 1914 and 1919, is an outstanding example of Byzantine-inspired architecture.

The famous triple arched Romanesque portal, a memorial to Cornelius Vanderbilt II, was designed by Stamford White of the famous architectural practice of McKim, Mead & White in 1900. It formed part of the previous church of this Episcopal congregation on Madison Square, and was moved to Park Avenue and incorporated in the present building some 17 years later.

The church is constructed of salmon-colored brick and limestone in contrasting bands. Many of the carvings on the facade represent the life of Saint Bartholomew.

The bronze entrance doors and carved panels are the work of several sculptors: Daniel C. French and Andrew O'Connor the central bay, Herbert Adams the left bay, and Philip Martiny the right bay. The design of the entrance portico was modeled on the Romanesque church of St. Gilles du Gard, near Arles in France.

Architect Bertram Goodhue
Built 1914–1919

60

26. St. Patrick's Cathedral

Fifth Avenue at 50th Street

The City of New York was made an archdiocese in 1850, and the Archbishop, John Hughes, proposed to build the Cathedral on a plot of land owned by the church, although at the time the location of the site was considered too far up town, away from the center.

The Cathedral was built over many years to the Neo-Gothic design of architect James Renwick Jr. Construction started in 1853, and the bulk of the work was completed by 1878; the 330-feet-high spires were a later addition, completed in 1888.

The Lady Chapel at the eastern end of the Cathedral, designed in the French Gothic Eclectic style by Charles T. Matthews, was completed in 1906. The complex now also includes the Rectory and the Cardinal's residence.

St. Patrick's is the largest Roman Catholic Cathedral in the United States. The exterior is white marble with characteristic Gothic arches, opulent stained-glass windows, and laced stonework. Massive bronze doors decorated with the statues of the saints of New York give access to the interior which has a seating capacity of some 2,500.

In 1965 Pope Paul VI visited the Cathedral on the first papal journey to the United States.

Architect James Renwick Jr.
Built 1853–1878

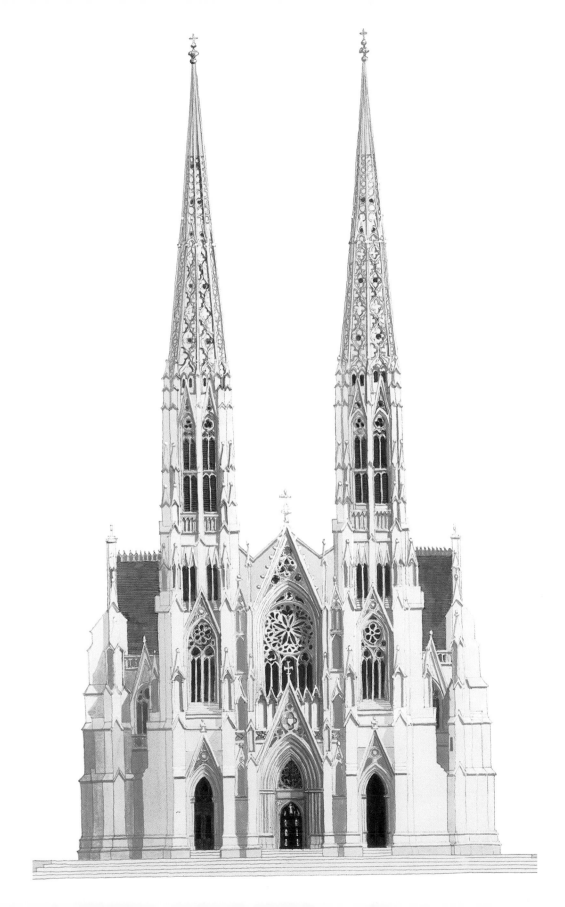

63

27. CENTRAL SYNAGOGUE
652 LEXINGTON AVENUE

As the city's population began to shift northwards, the congregation purchased the plot of land on the corner of Lexington Avenue and 55th Street and commissioned the Prussian born Jewish architect, Henry Fernbach, to design the new sanctuary. Reflecting the outcome of the debate on the form of designs for synagogues in the 19th century, the architect followed the Moorish-inspired style which had taken root in Germany and which reflected the tradition of the Jews in Moorish Spain.

The synagogue is the oldest building in New York State in continuous use by a Jewish congregation.

The local brownstone-faced Central Synagogue, with banded horseshoe arches above the doors and windows and twin towers rising 122 feet to the top of the onion-shaped green copper domes, is considered to be the best example of Moorish-Islamic Revival architecture. It was restored in 1995.

Architect Henry Fernbach
Completed 1870

28. Carnegie Hall
Seventh Avenue at 57th Street

In 1890 the Scottish immigrant Andrew Carnegie, industrialist and philanthropist, financed the building of Carnegie Hall as part of his efforts for "the improvement of mankind". The architect William B. Tuthill designed the Hall. He was inspired by the Italian Renaissance style and faced the building in Roman brick and decorated terracotta. The tower was added later, as was the studio wing which was built in 1896, the work of H.J. Hardenbergh.

Peter Ilyich Tchaikovsky, on his American conducting debut, gave the opening concert with the performance of his *Marche Solenelle*. Over the years he has been followed by such diverse artists as Arturo Toscanini, Leonard Bernstein, Ella Fitzgerald and the Beatles. The excellent acoustics of the concert hall are attributed to the curved balconies, the shape of the ceiling, and the velvet coverings which absorb echoes. In the 1960s the Hall was threatened with demolition, but support from the artists and performers, led by the violinist Isaac Stern, saved the building and funds were raised to renovate the interior.

The Way to Carnegie Hall

I was very young and a stranger to midtown Manhattan, walking along 57th Street, kind of lost, when I saw a man with a violin case and thought he could help me. "How do I get to Carnegie Hall?" I asked. And he answered, "Practice, practice!" Of course that never really happened to me, but it is the most famous story about the most famous concert hall in the world. I thought of it some years ago as I stood on the stage of that hallowed hall, doing a 'stand-up' for a TV program. I was no Heifetz or Horowitz or Toscanini, I told myself as I stood there, the only audience my camera crew. But I had gotten to Carnegie Hall!

Leonard Harris, author

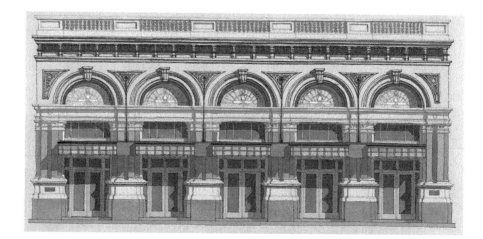

Architect William B. Tuthill
Built 1889–1897

29. GAINSBOROUGH STUDIOS
222 CENTRAL PARK SOUTH

The building was designed by the architect Charles W. Buckham in 1907 as a combined studio and living accommodation for artists. The double height windows of the studios face north and look over Central Park, while the apartments are at the back. The bust of Thomas Gainsborough decorates the front, above a frieze by Isidore Konti entitled 'A festival procession of the arts'. The decorative tile mural came from the Moravian Tile Works of Henry Mercer. The facade was restored in 1988 and it is one of my favorite quirky buildings, extra memorable for me because it took so many trips to New York before I was able to see the whole building without scaffolding. I wonder how many of the studios are occupied by working artists nowadays?

Architect Charles W. Buckham
Built 1907

30. METROPOLITAN OPERA HOUSE

LINCOLN CENTER
COLUMBUS AVENUE AT 64TH STREET

The Metropolitan Opera House is part of the Lincoln Center complex dedicated to the performing arts. The buildings surround the rectangular plaza which is elevated above and open to Columbus Avenue. The three buildings with flat roofs and colonnades are covered in white marble and arranged in an austere classical layout and style.

The approach, up a long low set of steps from Columbus Avenue, leads directly ahead to the Metropolitan Opera House which was built in 1966 to the design of the architect Wallace K. Harrison. On the left is the New York State Theater, built in 1964; on the right is the Avery Fisher Hall, built in 1962.

Behind the impressive tall arches of the Metropolitan Opera House is the sumptuous lobby which is dominated by two large and splendid murals by Marc Chagall.

The whole complex is best appreciated at night when the buildings and fountain are illuminated.

LOVE AT LAST
The Metropolitan Opera and I met in 1966, but it wasn't love for nearly 24 years. I was looking good in black tie in September '66, and the new house was looking splendid on its opening night at the Lincoln Center. The opera, *Cleopatra*, by Samuel Barber, was not quite so splendid and the Met and I really didn't hit it off, though we saw each other from time to time over the years. Then came that night in January of 1990. The opera was *Tosca*, and before I could set up my defences, Pavarotti smote me with 'Recondita Armonia'. By the time the evening was over, Scarpia, Cavaradossi, Tosca and I had all fallen.   *George C. Spelvin, theater critic, New York*

Architect Wallace K. Harrison
Opened 1966

THE SMELL OF GREASE PAINT

In its 116-year history, the Metropolitan Opera has had two homes. When the company moved from its original theater on Broadway and 39th Street to its new one at Lincoln Center, the common way to differentiate between the two was 'Old Met' and 'New Met'. Now, 33 years later, it seems odd to talk about a 'New Met'. No building can stay new forever.

The Old Met was demolished in 1967, shortly after the company's first performances in its new home. I am a lover of old theaters, and after all these years I am sorry that I never had a chance to see this one, much less to hear a performance in it. In my work, I've spent many hours pouring over photographs of its interior and exterior, and feel I know it as well as one can know a building one has never set foot in. No photograph taken after the 19th century makes the exterior look attractive and most of the theater's lobby areas look drab, but one can understand why the Old Met's auditorium was long considered one of the glories of New York.

The auditorium of the Met's current home is likewise its most successful feature. The building may be permanently stuck in 1966, but the interior seems to have aged better than the facade. I like it best when I show it to people who have never seen it before: the Austrian crystal chandeliers still have the ability to inspire wonder – whether they're standing still or ascending, as they do before each performance – and the red-and-gold color scheme, brought over from the old house gives the auditorium a warmth that the rest of the building lacks. Depending on where one sits, the theater's size and shape can make the stage and everything that takes place on it seem incidental to the rest of the room; on the other hand, I've been to enough great performances there to know that the right singers can make this 3,800-seat house seem like a salon.

Paul Gruber, Executive Director, Metropolitan Opera Guild

Old Metropolitan Opera House (now demolished)

31. LOTOS CLUB
5 EAST 66TH STREET

How splendid it must be to have a mother generous and rich enough to be able to give her daughters a house each. So it was that Mrs Elliott F. Shepard gave Edith, married to Ernesto Fabbri, their house, and to her other daughter, Maria Louisa, the wife of William J. Schiefflin, this house, specially designed and built for them. Mrs. Elliott F. Shepard, daughter of William H. Vanderbilt, employed the family's favorite architect Richard Howland Hunt to design the house. The building, known as the Schiefflin House, thus represented the style and taste of an old American aristocratic family and huge amounts of new Vanderbilt money.

The five-story-high building in brick and limestone, with a rusticated ground floor and elaborate mansard roofing, in a typical French bourgeoisie style, was built at the end of the 1890s.

The architects used the latest technology to fireproof the building, and its steel frame allowed the floors to bear the weight of the hundreds of people attending celebrations in the house.

The splendid formal staircase leads to the upper floors, accommodating the library and a banqueting room with a colossal fireplace sculpted by Karl Bitter.

Young journalists founded the Lotos Club in 1870 to support literature, and moved into the house in 1947.

Architect Richard Howland Hunt
Built late 1890s

32. FRICK COLLECTION
1 EAST 70TH STREET

This part of Fifth Avenue used to be called Millionaire's Row, but many of the grand houses have now been demolished and replaced by apartment blocks. A few do remain, converted for use by institutions. The Frick Collection is the one exception, remaining as it was when the first and only owner, Henry Clay Frick (1849–1919), left it.

The mansion was designed in 1913 by Thomas Hastings as both a residence and a gallery to display the great art collection of the owner. Occupying an entire city block along Fifth Avenue, the house is set back on a terraced garden behind a retaining wall. The style of the mansion is that of Louis XV. It comprises the private apartments of the family, an interior court with its fountain and plants and a half story picture gallery, the largest in a private house in the city. The wealth to build such a palace was created by Henry Frick and considerably enlarged in association with the Carnegie, Phipps & Company steel works.

After Frick's death the house and its priceless art collection was left to the nation. The building was enlarged and opened to the public in 1935. The special fascination of this unique collection lies in the fact that it is displayed in a residential setting with furniture, curtains at the windows, open fireplaces and bell pushes set discreetly in paneled walls to summon the servants.

Architect Carrère and Hastings
Built 1913

33. BETHESDA FOUNTAIN

CENTRAL PARK
AT 72ND STREET

Central Park is a product of the long-term vision of mid-19th century New York citizens. Over a period of some 20 years 750 acres of central Manhattan Island were refashioned: swamps were drained, rocks moved, and thousands upon thousands of trees planted. The scheme for the Park was masterminded by Frederick Law Olmsted, an engineer and landscape architect, who teamed up with the English-born architect Calvert Vaux.

Bethesda Fountain commemorates those in the navy who died in the Civil War. It is a key architectural feature of Central Park, and was dedicated in 1873. The fountain is named after the biblical account of a healing angel at the pool of Bethesda in Jerusalem.

The fountain stands on a richly ornamented Spanish-style terrace, the work of Jacob Rey Mould, and overlooks the Lake and the Ramble – a wooded stretch of some thirty-seven acres, a paradise for bird lovers.

The winged 'Angel of the Waters' standing on an elevated bowl supported by a cluster of cherubim is by Emma Stebbins, the first woman to receive a civic commisison in New York City. The statue was originally commissioned to mark the opening of the Croton Aqueduct system in 1842, bringing the city its first supply of pure water.

Architect Jacob Rey Mould
Built 1873

34. DAKOTA APARTMENTS
1 WEST 72ND STREET
AT CENTRAL PARK WEST

Edward Clark, lawyer, director of the Singer Sewing Machine Company, and speculator, purchased this piece of land beside Central Park in 1877, long before the area was thought to be suitable for development. European capitals had for a long time had luxurious apartment blocks, but these were still unknown to New York until Clark decided to build one.

In 1880 the architect Edward J. Hardenbergh was commissioned to design a spectacular apartment house with the interior to include every comfort and luxury available at the time.

In 1884, the year that the Dakota Building was finished, its location was so far north of what was then considered civilized New York that it was said it might as well be in Dakota – hence the name, which has stuck.

Influenced by German and French Renaissance style, the picturesque steeply-pitched roofs are covered with dormer windows. The Dakota has 65 apartments some with four rooms, some with 20. Originally conceived as a family hotel, the tenants could use the main dining room or eat in their own apartments. The rooms were all finished to a high degree of luxury with paneled walls. There were four elevators, one in each corner of the inner courtyard, a private electric generator to supply power, and the most up-to-date fire prevention devices.

To build such a large and expensive building this far north was at the time a considerable gamble, but it turned out to be a great success and the first of many such apartment blocks built in the area. The Dakota has been home to the rich and the

famous ever since. Amongst its 20th century residents have been Lauren Bacall, Leonard Bernstein, Judy Garland and Roberta Flack. John and Yoko Lennon brought particular fame to the building, especially when John Lennon was murdered outside the entrance in 1980.

Architect Edward J. Hardenbergh
Completed 1884

35. AMERICAN MUSEUM OF NATURAL HISTORY

CENTRAL PARK WEST AT 77TH STREET

As with many large and complex buildings, this Museum was built over many years and consequently represents several styles of construction. The first building was put up in 1874–77, designed by architects Vaux & Mould, and the most recent addition, the new Planetarium, by architects Polshek & Partners, was begun as recently as 1997. The full site of the Museum extends over an area of about 18 acres.

The pink granite Romanesque Revival facade on West 77th Street contrasts strongly with the main entrance to the Museum facing on to Central Park. This is in the form of a massive triumphal arch surmounting an equestrian statue of Theodore Roosevelt by James Earle Fraser, erected in 1939.

The collection housed in the Museum was started in 1874 and now includes some 34 million items. It interprets its theme in very diverse forms, ranging from animal dioramas, model Indian villages, crafts, costumes and jewelry to other artefacts of the peoples of pre-colonial Americas.

Architects: Calvert Vaux & J. Wrey Mould 1874–1877
South and part West elevation Cady, Berg & See 1888–1908
East wing Trowbridge & Livingston 1912–1934
Theodore Roosevelt Memorial Hall John Russell Pope 1931–1934
Library Kevin Roche John Dinkeloo Associates 1900–1992
Hayden Planetarium Polshek & Partners 1997–2000

36. METROPOLITAN MUSEUM OF ART

1000 FIFTH AVENUE
AT 82ND STREET

The first building on this site was erected in 1870. Opened by President Rutherford Hayes it was a high Victorian Gothic building set back from Fifth Avenue. It is now only partially visible in the interior of the Museum.

The present central facade, with entrance arches and incomplete stone block sculptural groups above the paired Corinthian columns, was designed by Richard Morris Hunt and completed by his son in 1895. Many more additions followed, the latest completed in 1990, which make the Metropolitan the largest museum in the western hemisphere. As well as the addition of new wings, incorporated into the complex are parts of several historic buildings conserved specially for this purpose.

Part of the American Wing is the old Assay Office from Wall Street, while the Library facade is from the Madison Square Presbyterian Church.

The building and the land are owned by the City and the collections are held in trust by the Museum Trustees. The most generous benefactor, J. Pierpoint Morgan, gave his collection, valued at $60 million in 1913.

The ever-changing special exhibitions and display of art and artifacts, lectures, concerts, film shows and discussions attract visitors from around the world. The grand steps up to the entrance are a popular place to meet and to rest after visiting the Museum, especially on a sunny day.

Architect Richard Morris Hunt
Completed 1902

LOST FOR A DAY

I can lose myself for a whole day in the Museum. I might visit the armor room, quiet and empty, and walk among the beautiful metallic shapes which reflect light as I move around the room, the heraldic images still marking imaginary territory. Then perhaps I look at photography and painting to notice how various artists from different time periods have handled light, all of which relates to my work as an artist. A visit is never complete without seeing some treasures from old kingdom Egypt. So many choices which always provide something for the senses. As I leave, I feel replenished and eager to get back to my own work in the studio.

Deborah Remington, artist

37. SOLOMON R. GUGGENHEIM MUSEUM
1071 FIFTH AVENUE AT 89TH STREET

This splendid and extraordinary structure is Frank Lloyd Wright's only building in New York City, and is considered to be one of the architect's major achievements. Opened in October 1959, the design and construction took over 16 years to complete due to the many changes required to accommodate strict building codes.

Shaped like a giant white shell, the all-white concrete surfaces of the spiral exterior are in complete contrast to the conservative apartment buildings along Fifth Avenue. The recessed spiral of the central hall, lit by a domed skylight some 90 feet above, is intended to reflect natural shapes from Central Park across the Avenue. The interior layout has its own very practical logic: visitors take the lift to the top and walk down the spiral ramp, viewing the collection at a leisurely pace on the way.

Commissioned by the copper magnate, Solomon R. Guggenheim, to exhibit his collection of non-objective and abstract art, the Museum now hosts regular exhibitions of work by contemporary artists as well as by the 'classics' of the modern art establishment.

Architect Frank Lloyd Wright
Completed 1959

THE SOLOMON R GUGGENHEIM MUSEUM

THE GUGGENHEIM ADVENTURE

The journey begins in a small lift which travels to the very top of the building and from then on it is downhill. The lift doors open on to a unique space, flooded with light from a huge window above. Immediately the path is formed by a ramp which wraps around the outer edge of the diminishing spiral, past the exhibition hung on the outer wall. It is hard to remember the display as the building distracts and surprises, looking different from every angle. Reaching the bottom and looking up into the magnificent void is so exhilarating – the lure of the lift is impossible to resist.

The lift doors open again at the top and the impulse is to go to the edge and look down into the void. This experience is not recommended for anyone with vertigo. The balustrade leans away to the centre, fighting the centrifugal refuge of the ramp. Holding on very tightly, there is a fascinating conflict to be seen. The solid form and determined descent of the ramp contrasts with people moving haphazardly, unaware of the manipulative circulation of the building. Turning away from the ramp there are other intriguing spaces to discover, amongst them, the triangular loos. Then imperceptibly the end of the ramp meets the ground floor. Once again the exhibition is eclipsed by the adventure. *Demetra Ryder Runton, architect*

38. COOPER-HEWITT MUSEUM

2 EAST 91ST STREET

This sumptuous mansion was built as the home of Andrew Carnegie on land that at the time of purchase was fit only for goats. Carnegie was wealthy on a fabulous scale – he received $250 million for the sale of his steel company in 1901. His 64-room house was designed with Georgian-inspired brickwork and Beaux-Arts ornamentation around the most up to date structural and mechanical systems of the day. Unlike the neighboring grand buildings, a large garden and landscaped grounds act as buffer to the surrounding city. Carnegie could afford to indulge himself.

In 1972 the property became part of the Smithsonian Institution and was converted to house the decorative art collections of Peter Cooper (founder of Cooper Union) and his granddaughters Eleanor and Sarah Hewitt. As its subtitle, the National Museum of Design, suggests, it incorporates furniture, wallpaper, glassware, ceramics, and textiles, together with an extensive and important collection of old master drawings.

Architects Babb, Cook & Willard
Built 1899–1903

39. JEWISH MUSEUM

1109 FIFTH AVENUE AT 92ND STREET

The house was built for the banker Felix Warburg and his wife Frieda Schiff, who wanted a six-story residence on the corner of the avenue with a large garden to the side. The architect commissioned was Cass Gilbert, well known for his designs in the style of Francis I of France. The limestone-faced mansion, inspired by the châteaux of the Loire Valley, was completed in 1908.

The rooms on the first floor facing the park displayed a collection of early German and Italian woodcuts and etchings. On the second floor, where all the rooms opened on to each other, was the music room with grand piano and an Aeolian pipe organ, and a sitting room displaying a collection of Italian paintings. Next to this were the conservatory and the dining room which was used for formal occasions. The third floor was for the use of the family, with sitting and dining rooms and the master bedroom. The children lived on the fourth floor, guests on the fifth, and staff in the attic. After the death of Felix Warburg, his widow presented the house to the Jewish Museum in 1944.

Architect Cass Gilbert
Completed 1908

4 East 74th Street. I drew this charming little house, partly to show that New York
is not all skyscrapers, but also because I like its bourgeois domestic character

SELECT BIBLIOGRAPHY

Beaux-Art Architecture in New York – A Photographic Guide,
Henry Hope Reed, Dover Publications

The Companion Guide to New York,
Michael Leapman, Companion Guides

Elegant New York – The Builders and Their Buildings 1885–1915,
John Tauranac and Christopher Little, Abbeville Press

Guide to New York City Landmarks,
Andrew S. Dolkart for the NY City Landmarks Preservation Commission,
John Wiley

New York – Eyewitness Travel Guide,
Eleanor Berman, Dorling Kindersley

New York for New Yorkers – A Historical Treasury and Guide to the Buildings and Monuments of Manhattan,
Liza M. Green, W.W. Norton & Company

New York NY – American Express Pocket Guide,
Herbert Bailey Livesey, Mitchell Beazley

NY Landmarks – Collection of Architectural and Historical Details,
Charles J. Ziga, Dovetail Books

The importance of Berlin has changed from being on the front line between the opposing armies of NATO and the Warsaw Pact, to becoming once again the capital city of a reunited Germany.

Most of the city's buildings are now either new or restored. In the last ten years entire new districts have grown up on the site of what was once the infamous Berlin Wall. The illustrations include the Reichstag with its new glass dome, museums and churches around the Unter den Linden and on Museum Island, the restored old districts just north and east of the centre, government buildings and the gleaming new development around Potsdamer Platz. All these make Berlin an exciting and changing city for those interested in architecture. The book illustrates some forty of these buildings, with a short description accompanying each, including details of its architecture and dates of construction or reconstruction.

ISBN 1 85149 362 X
96pp., 90 colour illustrations
9¾ x 7¾in./247 x 196mm
£9.50/$12.50

Although he trained as an architect, Andras Kaldor's love of the opera has proved the stronger influence and he has spent the last twelve years painting major opera houses around the world. He has visited all of the houses illustrated in this book.

The façade of each opera house is illustrated in all its splendour. The drawings are first done in pen and ink in architectural style, with scrupulous attention to detail. They are then painted in gouache. The effect is stunning and allows the viewer to experience the complexity and exuberance of these flamboyant 18th, 19th and 20th century buildings. In addition to the façades the artist has added many detailed drawings of particular aspects of the exteriors and interiors of the buildings. Anecdotal text accompanying the opera houses is written by well-known personalities who have a personal association with the individual house. Background details of the history, architecture, composers, operas, and singers are also given.

Many of these opera houses, such as Covent Garden, the Bolshoi Theatre, the Opéra Comique, the Sydney Opera House, the Metropolitan in New York and the San Francisco Opera House, are household names known the world over.

ISBN 1 85149 363 8
129pp., colour throughout
9¾ x 7¾in./247 x 196mm
£9.50/$14.95

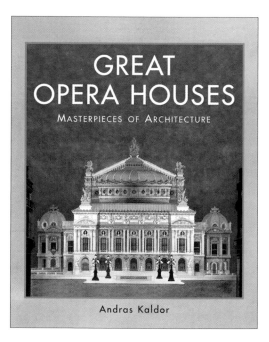

Andras Kaldor, seen here in his gallery in Dartmouth, England, surrounded by some of his architectural paintings. In his art he successfully combines the disciplines of painting and architecture. He has portrayed famous buildings and monuments from Berlin to San Francisco and his works have been exhibited on both sides of the Atlantic.

Andras Kaldor, 15 Newcomen Road, Dartmouth, Devon TQ6 9BN
Telephone 01803 833874 Fax: 01803 835161
www.kaldor.co.uk
email: andras@kaldor.co.uk